Module 10: Numeracy

Introduction

Numeracy is an essential skill for everyone. In everyday life, we need mathematics to help us solve problems and make decisions; for example, we may wish to manage our finances, make plans for travel or organise a social event. To make a positive contribution to society and the wider world, we need to make sense of how our economy works and understand the facts and figures that are presented in news reports.

Numeracy is also important for studying in higher education where it will be necessary to read academic papers and carry out investigations that involve data collection and analysis. Moving into the workplace afterwards requires the continued use of mathematics in a wide range of fields including healthcare, business, politics, science and law.

Contents

1 Working with numbers

At the end of this unit, you will be able to:

- learn how to work with fractions
- understand the meaning of percentages
- use decimal numbers in calculations

Task 1 Simplifying fractions

When we simplify a fraction, we are trying to write the fraction in its smallest form without changing its value.

$\frac{5}{10}$

□□□□□ □□□□□   has the same value as $\frac{1}{2}$ □□

To simplify a fraction, try to divide the top and bottom by the same number; repeat this process until it cannot be done again and the fraction will be written in its simplest form.

Remember, you must use the same number for dividing each part of the fraction.

> **Example**
> Simplify $\frac{100}{400}$.
>
> $\frac{100}{400}$ divide by 10 $\frac{10}{40}$ divide by 2 $\frac{5}{20}$ divide by 5 $\frac{1}{4}$
>
> So, $\frac{100}{400}$ in its simplest form is $\frac{1}{4}$.

1.1 **Write each of the fractions in its smallest form.**

a. $\frac{60}{100}$ b. $\frac{13}{22}$ c. $\frac{9}{81}$

1.2 **Circle the fraction that shows $\frac{64}{144}$ in its simplest form.**

a. $\frac{64}{144}$

b. $\frac{4}{9}$

c. $\frac{16}{36}$

d. $\frac{8}{18}$

Task 2 Using fractions in practice

There are two steps needed to find a fraction of an amount:

Step 1: Divide the amount by the bottom of the fraction.
Step 2: Multiply your result by the top of the fraction.

> **Example**
>
> Find $\frac{3}{7}$ of 56.
>
> Step 1: 56 divided by 7 is 8.
> Step 2: Multiplying 8 by 3 gives 24.
> So, $\frac{3}{7}$ of 56 = 24.

2.1 **Without using a calculator, find:**

a. $\frac{2}{9}$ of 45

b. $\frac{4}{5}$ of 120

Task 3 Finding a percentage of a quantity

There are two steps needed to find the percentage of a quantity:

Step 1: Find 1% by dividing the quantity by 100.
Step 2: Multiply the result from step 1 by the percentage you are trying to find.

> **Example**
>
> Find 30% of 500.
>
> Step 1: 500 divided by 100 is 5, so 1% of 500 is 5.
> Step 2: Multiplying 5 by 30 gives 150.
> So, 30% of 500 = 150.

3.1 **Find each of the following percentages of 160.**

a.   10%

b.   55%

c.   80%

3.2 There are 200 passengers on an airliner that departs from a London airport. The check-in records show that 48% of the passengers are men, 33% are women and 19% are children.

Work out the number of men, women and children travelling as passengers on the airliner.

Task 4 Percentage increase and decrease

Starting with a basic quantity, we sometimes need to find out its new value when it is increased or decreased by a specific percentage.

Example
The price of a cinema ticket is £9.60, but next month it will be increased by 5%. How much will a cinema ticket cost next month?
Finding 5% of £9.60 gives 48p.
The new ticket price is £9.60 + 48p = £10.08.

Example
In an advertisement, an electrical store announces that prices will be reduced by 20% for a week. If the current price of a television is £350, calculate its sale price.
Finding 20% of £350 gives £70.
The sale price will be £350 – £70 = £280.

4.1 Calculate the new quantity when:

a.   150 kg is decreased by 30%

b.   64 cm is increased by 25%

4.2 A recipe book written by a well-known chef can be ordered on a bookstore website, or can be bought in a high-street bookshop. The prices are listed as:

purchasing choice	advertised price	sale price
high-street bookshop	£25	reduced by 35%
online bookstore	£18	reduced by 5%

Using the sale prices, which purchasing choice is more expensive?

Task 5 Types of decimal number

There are three types of decimal number:

1. **Exact:** The decimal part of the number has a finite number of digits.

   0.7

   266.45

   5.89142

2. **Recurring:** Some digits in the decimal part of the number are repeated endlessly.

   0.333333 …

   36.519519519 …

   4.134727272 …

3. **Not exact and non-recurrent:** There are an endless number of digits in the decimal part of the number and it does not have digits which are repeated in a pattern.

   3.1415926535 … (also known as Pi, denoted π)

   1.6180339887 … (also known as the golden ratio, denoted φ)

5.1 Are the statements true (T) or false (F)?

   a. 3.678888888 … is a recurring decimal number. ☐

   b. 0.259876 is a decimal number that is not exact and non-recurrent. ☐

   c. 4465.87555411025 is an exact decimal number. ☐

Task 6 Adding and subtracting decimal numbers

Before we can add or subtract decimal numbers, we must first line up the decimal points and then fill any empty spaces with a zero. Then we can add or subtract as if we were handling whole numbers, making sure there is a decimal point located in the correct place in the answer.

Example
Add 65.82, 2.3 and 124.

```
      6 5 . 8 2
          2 . 3      ← line up the decimal
  +  1 2 4 .              points

      0 6 5 . 8 2
      0 0 2 . 3 0    ← fill any empty spaces
  +  1 2 4 . 0 0         with a zero

      0 6 5 . 8 2
      0 0 2 . 3 0
      1 2 4 . 0 0
  +  1 9 2 . 1 2    ← locate the decimal point
                        correctly in the answer
```

Example
Subtract 2.365 from 94.1.

```
      9 4 . 1
  –       2 . 3 6 5  ← line up the decimal points

      9 4 . 1 0 0   ← fill any empty spaces with
  –  0 2 . 3 6 5       a zero

      9 4 . 1 0 0
  –  0 2 . 3 6 5
      9 1 . 7 3 5   ← locate the decimal point
                       correctly in the answer
```

6.1 Add the following sets of decimal numbers.

a.   233.7 + 89 + 1.55

b.   16.529 + 427.6 + 5.93

6.2 Complete these subtractions without using a calculator.

a.   552.9 – 63.327

b.   9.5 – 2.8754

Reflect

Put these values in the correct numerical order, starting with the smallest in the list and ending with the largest.

a.   90% of 30   20% of 75   5% of 60   50% of 44

b.   970 – 45.38   65.298 + 1.2 + 397   55.7 – 3.441

2 What is *statistics*?

At the end of this unit, you will be able to:
- understand the purpose of statistics
- recognise different types of variables

Task 1 What is *statistics*?

Statistics is a mathematical science that generally involves using information in four stages of work:

1. Collection – taking measurements, making observations and asking questions.
2. Analysis – using diagrams and numerical values to highlight interesting features.
3. Interpretation – making comparisons and reaching conclusions.
4. Presentation – writing a report or giving a verbal presentation to share our conclusions.

1.1 Match the stages of work above (1–4) with the activities (a–d).

a. After we have finished an investigation we tell people the results in an article uploaded to a sporting website. ☐

b. We identify the most popular team sport in which people participate. ☐

c. During an interview, we ask people questions about their weekly exercise routine. ☐

d. We make a comparison between males and females to establish which gender spends the most time competing in sporting events. ☐

1.2 Choose a magazine or newspaper article that describes the results of an opinion poll. Read the article carefully and write a short paragraph in response to each question.

a. How was information collected and from whom?

b. Did the writer highlight any interesting patterns or features in the information?

c. Were comparisons made between different groups of people?

d. Did the writer provide graphs and charts to present the information?

Task 2 Data for different subjects

Information, also known as data, is collected and presented for a wide range of subject areas. For example, in education, we might be interested in information such as:
- the percentage of students who pass an exam
- the number of times a student is absent from class
- the most popular subject studied at college

2.1 With a partner, consider each of the subject areas and write down some examples of information that are likely to be of interest.

a. healthcare

b. politics

c. business

2

Task 3 Variable types

A *variable* is a characteristic or an attribute that can have different values. Every variable can be described as *quantitative* or *qualitative* depending on what the information means.

Qualitative variables represent a characteristic that cannot be described using numbers; letters or words are used instead.

> Example
> The colour of cars parked in a street (red or blue or silver).

Quantitative variables can be counted or measured on a numerical scale; their values can always be expressed as a number.

> Example
> The number of students in a class (30 or 18 or 124).

Quantitative variables can also be classified as *discrete* or *continuous*.

A *discrete variable* can only take specific numbers; its values can usually be counted

> Example
> The number of customers in a queue (3 or 10 or 6).

A *continuous variable* can take any value within a specific range, these variables usually involve measurements.

> Example
> The height of buildings in a city (188.1 m or 111.3 m or 41.0 m).

3.1 **Determine whether the following variables are *quantitative* or *qualitative*.**

    a.   Colour of dresses in a clothes shop.   _____

    b.   Preferred hot drink of people in a hotel.   _____

    c.   Number of biscuits in a packet.   _____

    d.   Number of pencils in a box.   _____

3.2 **Are the statements true (T) or false (F)? Try to give a reason for each response.**

    a.   Weight of crisps in a bag is a continuous variable.   ☐

    b.   Nationality of people visiting a museum is a discrete variable.   ☐

    c.   Number of letters in a post box is a continuous variable.   ☐

    d.   Number of apples in a fruit bowl is a discrete variable.   ☐

3.3 The data in the table were collected about a friend's dog called Curtis. In each case, classify the information.

variable	data	quantitative or qualitative?	discrete or continuous or neither?
breed	greyhound		
length of tail	33 cm		
number of walks in a week	14		
colour	black		
weight	32.5 kg		
number of toys owned	8		

3.4 Write down your own ideas for three variables that are:

a. qualitative

_____

b. quantitative and discrete

_____

c. quantitative and continuous

_____

Reflect

Using an international news website, find an article that includes some numerical data.

Describe how the reporter uses statistics to support their ideas and make a list of the data provided.

Collecting data

At the end of this unit, you will be able to:

- understand why sample data is used
- learn how to write a questionnaire
- use interview questions to collect different types of data

Task 1 Populations and samples

When you carry out an investigation to find out information about a group of people, this group is known as the *population*; it is the entire set of people from whom we wish to collect information.

> **Example**
> All of the visitors to a museum.

If the population is very large then it is usually time-consuming and expensive to ask for information from every member. Instead you could decide to contact a small group of the people selected from the population; this smaller group of people is called a *sample*.

> **Example**
> Visitors to a museum who are aged 10.

1.1 **Would it be practical to contact every member of the population for each of the investigations?**

    a.   Finding out the favourite colour of all adults who live in London.

    b.   Finding out the height of each employee working in one office location.

    c.   Finding out the annual salary of all women who work full-time in the UK.

1.2 **With a partner, discuss the advantages of choosing a sample for data collection compared to asking every member of a population for information.**

1.3 **A large company with offices in many countries wants to find out whether its employees travel to work each day by car, train, bicycle, bus or by walking. It is impractical and expensive to ask every employee, so it is decided that only the employees in the New York office will be asked.**

    In this scenario, which group is the population and which group is the sample?

    a.   population _____

    b.   sample _____

Task 2 Bias in sampling

If you collect data using a sample, then you must ensure that the people you include in the sample are representative of the entire population. Otherwise, it won't be possible to reach conclusions about the population based on sample information. A sample is *biased* if it isn't representative of the population from which it was chosen.

2.1 **Read the two investigations. With a partner, decide why the proposed sample might be biased.**

    a. Investigation: People's opinion about whether they prefer to do their shopping in a large supermarket or prefer to visit small independent shops that each specialise in a specific type of product.

         Sample: People who are leaving the exit of a large supermarket with a trolley full of shopping.

    b. Investigation: The genre of film, such as horror, romance or comedy, preferred by teenagers when they go to the cinema with a group of friends at the weekend.

         Sample: Teenagers who have just purchased a ticket to see a horror film.

Task 3 Open and closed questions

Written questionnaires provide an efficient and inexpensive way of collecting data. The person who creates the questionnaire is often known as the researcher, and the person answering the questions is called a participant.

There are two types of questions that you can ask in a questionnaire – *open questions* and *closed questions*.

When a person answers an *open question*, they can give any response they choose. Open questions provide interesting information to the researcher, but they can be time consuming to complete for the participant.

> **Example**
>
> What is your opinion on extending school hours to include lessons at the weekend?

A *closed question* provides a fixed number of answers from which the participant must choose. Closed questions can be answered very quickly by the participant, but they do not provide information to the researcher about why a choice has been made.

> **Example**
>
> Would you like school lessons at the weekend?
>
> ☐ yes
>
> ☐ no
>
> ☐ not sure

3.1 **Read each question and decide whether it is an open question or a closed question.**

a.
> What do you think is the best way
> to revise for an examination?

_____

b.
> Put a (circle) around any of these activities
> that you did yesterday.
>
> reading   shopping   studying

_____

c.
> What is your age?
>
> ☐ under 18
>
> ☐ 18
>
> ☐ over 18

_____

d.
> **What is your opinion on global climate change?**

_____

3.2 **Work in small groups to discuss the benefits and problems of using open and closed questions in a questionnaire for:**

a.   the researcher

_____

b.   a participant

_____

Task 4 Types of interview questions

Interviews involve talking to each participant, asking them questions either face-to-face or by telephone. Carrying out interviews can be time-consuming, but the researcher will probably collect some very interesting information.

Questions used during an interview can usually be categorised into five groups depending on the information that the researcher is trying to investigate:

- current facts
- facts about past events
- general knowledge
- opinions
- feelings

4.1 **The following questions might be included in an interview about travel and tourism. In each case, determine to which group the question belongs.**

question	question group
Do you feel safe when you travel alone by train?	*feelings*
How many times did you travel overseas last year?	
Do you agree or disagree with this statement? *Tourism causes problems because demand for holiday homes makes housing too expensive for local people.*	
Which currency is used in Ecuador?	
Do you own a car?	

4.2 **Work with a partner to write down five questions that would be suitable for an interview about protecting rainforests. Make sure you include a question from each of the five groups.**

- _____
- _____
- _____
- _____
- _____

Reflect

Work with a partner to discuss the statements. Explain which ones apply to conducting an interview and which describe collecting information using an online questionnaire.

a. You can ask a complex question because it is possible to provide further explanation if a participant does not understand its meaning.

b. If a participant does not answer a question, the researcher will not know the reason why.

c. Responses can be reviewed and analysed quickly, sometimes using a computer package to help with a large amount of data.

Organising data using tables and calculations

At the end of this unit, you will be able to:
- use a frequency table for displaying data
- interpret two-way tables
- calculate averages

Task 1 Making a frequency table

The number of times that a specific value occurs in a set of data is known as its *frequency*. For both qualitative and quantitative variables, we can use a *frequency table* to display our collected data values and their corresponding frequencies.

Example

The children in a primary school class were asked to give their favourite school subject.
Their responses are shown below.

Mathematics	Art	Mathematics	Mathematics	Art
Art	Art	Science	History	Science
Science	Mathematics	Science	Geography	Mathematics
History	Science	Mathematics	Mathematics	Geography
Mathematics	Geography	Art	Geography	Science
Science	Art	Mathematics	Art	Science

The frequency table for this information is:

subject	frequency
Mathematics	9
Art	7
Science	8
History	2
Geography	4
total	**30**

Example

A football team recorded the number of goals that they scored in 20 matches:

| 1 | 2 | 0 | 0 | 3 | 1 | 0 | 1 | 2 | 2 | 2 | 1 | 0 | 0 | 0 | 3 | 2 | 4 | 1 | 3 |

The frequency table for this information is:

number of goals	frequency
0	6
1	5
2	5
3	3
4	1
total	**20**

1.1 College students were asked to say how many times they ate breakfast last week. Their responses are shown below. Construct a frequency table for this data.

7	4	1	2	3	3	6	6	5	3	7	1	1	2	4	7	4	1	2	3
0	2	2	3	7	7	4	1	6	3	6	3	2	7	4	1	1	2	1	7

1.2 Construct a frequency table to show the preferred hot drink for 20 customers in a café.

tea	coffee	hot chocolate	tea	coffee
coffee	tea	coffee	coffee	coffee
coffee	tea	tea	hot chocolate	hot chocolate
hot chocolate	tea	coffee	coffee	hot chocolate

1.3 The frequency table below shows the number of people queuing at each checkout in a supermarket.

number of customers	frequency
0	2
1	5
2	9
3	12
4	6
5	3

Use the table to decide whether the statements are true (T) or false (F). For false (F) statements, give the correct numerical value.

a. In total, there were 36 customers queuing at supermarket checkouts.

b. Sixteen checkouts had fewer than three customers in their queue.

c. There were 30 checkouts with more than two customers queuing.

4

Task 2 Two-way tables

In a *two-way table*, we display the frequency of values associated with two qualitative variables.

Example

A doctor is interested to find out whether his adult patients wear glasses or not. The information he collects is shown in the two-way table below.

		wears glasses			
		always	never	sometimes	**total**
gender	female	26	10	31	67
	male	17	22	8	47
	total	43	32	39	114

From this two-way table we can see that:
- The doctor asked 114 patients about wearing glasses.
- Only 17 male patients wear glasses all the time.
- In total, 32 of the doctor's patients never wear glasses.

2.1 Complete the sentences using information given in the two-way table which describes how school children usually travel to school each morning.

		travel to school			
		by car	by bus	by bicycle	walking	**total**
gender	girls	44	5	16	68	133
	boys	32	12	27	33	104
	total	76	17	43	101	237

a. In total, _____ children were asked about the way they usually travel to school.

b. The most popular way of travelling to school was _____.

c. More _____ than _____ took the bus to school.

d. More _____ than _____ gave a response to the question: 'How do you usually travel to school each morning?'

2.2 Construct a two-way table to display the following information that was collected when 160 adults were asked whether they would be voting in the next local election.

Out of 117 homeowners, 54 said that they would vote and 38 said that they would not vote; the remaining homeowners had not yet decided. In total, 63 of the adults said that they would vote; 16 of the adults who were not homeowners had not yet decided.

Task 3 Finding the mode, median and mean

An *average* identifies a typical value that is representative of a set of data you have collected. There are three types of average: the *mode*, the *median* and the *mean*.

The *mode* is the data value that occurs most frequently.

The *mean* is calculated as:

$$\frac{\text{sum of data values}}{\text{number of values collected}}$$

The *median* is the middle value for a set of data that has already been arranged in numerical order, from smallest to largest. If you have an odd number of data values, then the median is one of these values – it is the middle one. However, an even number of data values does not have an actual middle value, so we must find the mid-way point between the two values closest to the middle instead.

Example

In an end of term test, 15 students in a class achieved the following scores out of 30.

| 9 | 20 | 28 | 5 | 9 | 18 | 28 | 11 | 13 | 8 | 2 | 28 | 29 | 18 | 14 |

The mode for this data is 28 because this is the score that was recorded most frequently; three students achieved this score.

The sum of the data values is 240 and there are 15 students in the class, so the mean for this data is: 240 divided by 15 = 16.

Arranging the data values in numerical order gives:

| 2 | 5 | 8 | 9 | 9 | 11 | 13 | (14) | 18 | 18 | 20 | 28 | 28 | 28 | 29 |

The median is 14 because this is the score that is in the middle of the data.

If an extra student had joined the class, scoring 30, the data values in numerical order would now be:

| 2 | 5 | 8 | 9 | 9 | 11 | 13 | (14) | (18) | 18 | 20 | 28 | 28 | 28 | 29 | 30 |

The median now is 16, because this is the mid-way point between the two scores closest to the middle.

3.1 **The data values represent the number of items purchased in a supermarket by shoppers who use the self-service machines. Does this data have a mode? Give a reason for your response.**

| 10 | 9 | 4 | 18 | 5 | 6 | 8 | 12 | 11 | 7 | 15 | 3 |

_____

_____

_____

_____

_____

_____

3.2   Calculate the mean for the following sets of values.

a.

5	8	9	5	6	3	2	1	1	9	8	4	1	6	4	8

b.

24	36	21	18	16	36	74	52	27	19	29

3.3   The number of people living in each house on one street was recorded as:

5	3	1	2	4	3	4	5	6	2	2	1	1	3	5	4	4	5	1	3

Find the median for this set of data.

a.   not known   ☐

b.   2   ☐

c.   3   ☐

Reflect

Are the statements are true (T) or false (F)? Discuss your answers with a partner.

a.   We can calculate the mean for both quantitative and qualitative data.   ☐

b.   It is possible for a set of data to have more than one mode.   ☐

c.   The median and the mean will always be the same for a data set.   ☐

At the end of this unit, you will be able to:
- identify when to use pie charts and bar charts
- understand line graphs
- draw scatter diagrams for quantitative data
- avoid common mistakes with graphs and charts

Task 1 Pie charts

A pie chart is a circular diagram that is used for displaying proportions for qualitative data. The circle contains segments which represent each category as a percentage of the entire set of collected data. It is important to include a title and segment labels so that the meaning of the information presented in the pie chart is clear.

Example
This pie chart shows the responses from 200 people to the question, 'How often do you read non-fiction books?'

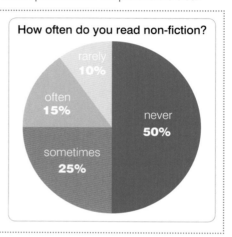

1.1 **Using the pie chart shown in the example above, decide whether the statements are true (T) or false (F).**

a. There were 25 people who said that they sometimes read non-fiction books.

b. More people responded with 'often' than with 'rarely'.

c. Twice as many people never read non-fiction books compared with those people who read them sometimes.

d. Only three people said that they often read non-fiction books.

1.2 **The pie chart below displays the answers received when an interviewer asked 80 people: 'Do you think recycling is important?' Describe two ways in which the presentation of this chart could be improved.**

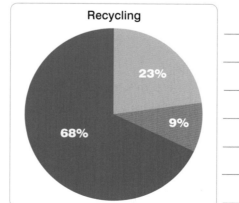

Task 2 Bar charts

Alternatively, qualitative data can be displayed using a bar chart in which each category in the data set is represented by a rectangular bar. Bars can be drawn vertically or horizontally, and the height or the length of a bar corresponds to the frequency of its category. Axes should be clearly labelled and you should always include a chart title. An alternative name for a bar chart is a column chart.

Example

In a questionnaire, girls in a shopping mall were asked about their favourite colour. The responses are shown in the bar charts below.

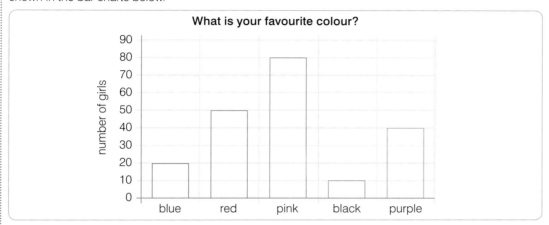

Displaying this bar chart with horizontal bars gives:

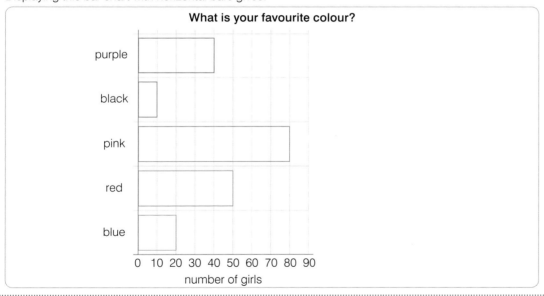

2.1 **Answer the questions using the information displayed in the example bar charts above.**

   a.   How many girls were asked about their favourite colour?   _____

   b.   Did more girls prefer blue compared to red?   _____

   c.   How many girls selected pink as their favourite colour?   _____

   d.   Which colour was the least popular?   _____

5

2.2 This table shows the different types of car that were sold by a dealership over a one-month period.

type of car	number sold
sports	32
luxury	15
family	57
hybrid	26
hatchback	49

a. Draw a bar chart with vertical bars to display this data.

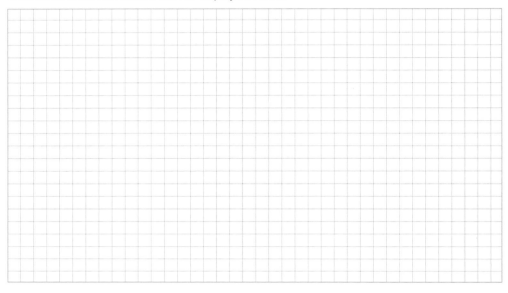

b. Draw another bar chart with horizontal bars to display this data. Then decide which presentation method you prefer.

Task 3 Line graphs

We would use a line graph to present quantitative data that changes over time. Each data value is plotted on the graph matching with its corresponding time period. Time is always shown on the horizontal axis and plotted points are usually joined with straight lines.

> **Example**
>
> In the line graph below, we can see how the number of students enrolled on a course has changed over a five-year period.
>
>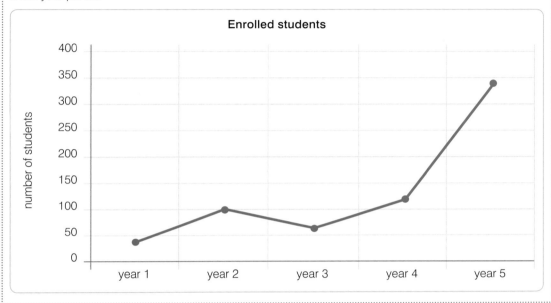

3.1 Using the line graph in the example above, write three sentences to describe how the number of enrolled students changed over time between years 1 to 5.

_____

_____

_____

_____

3.2 A researcher collects data from a group of students living in the same accommodation block. She asks them whether they find studying with friends 'more effective', 'less effective' or 'just the same' as studying alone. Would the researcher be able to use a line graph to display the results of her data collection? Why/Why not?

_____

_____

_____

_____

Task 4 Scatter diagrams

A scatter diagram is used to display information about two quantitative variables that might be connected in some way. Each plotted point represents a pair of numerical data values about the same person, but we do not join the data points with lines in a scatter diagram. Looking at the pattern of data values can tell us whether an increase in one variable is associated with an increase or a decrease in the other variable. Sometimes a scatter diagram shows that there is no relationship between the variables.

Example

This scatter diagram shows the relationship between height and weight for 12 women who attend a weekly fitness class.

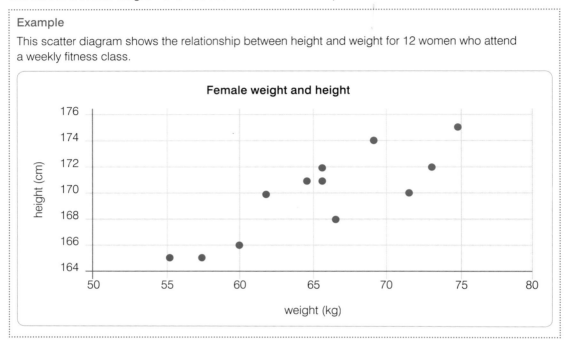

4.1 **For the women attending the weekly fitness class, what does the example scatter diagram show? Circle the correct answer.**

    a.   As height increases, weight increases.

    b.   As height increases, weight decreases.

    c.   There is no obvious relationship between height and weight.

4.2 Use the data given in the table to draw a scatter diagram to show the relationship between the exam and coursework scores for ten students. Plot the exam score on the horizontal axis and use the vertical axis for the coursework score.

exam score	80	15	92	64	37	55	41	76	32	89
coursework score	78	19	90	64	42	50	39	79	28	86

5

Task 5 Avoiding common mistakes

There are some common mistakes that researchers make when they are presenting their data using graphs and charts.

- When using a graph to present numerical data, it is important to label each axis clearly including any units of measurement when appropriate.
- If you choose to apply three-dimensional effects to a pie chart, you need to take care that the chart still provides an accurate representation of the information on which it is based.
- Try to avoid using unnecessary background images for your charts because this will distract the reader's attention from the data presented.

5.1 **For each pair of diagrams shown below, explain which diagram provides the best representation of the data set. Give a reason for each answer.**

a.

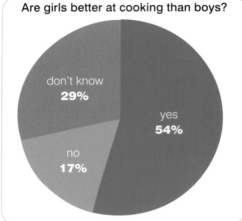

_____   _____

_____   _____

b.

_____   _____

_____   _____

5.2 Work with a partner to discuss and write down a set of five general guidelines that would help to ensure that all graphs and charts are well presented by researchers.

- _____
- _____
- _____
- _____
- _____

Reflect

Decide which diagram would be suitable for displaying the information listed below. In each case, choose a pie chart, a bar chart or a line graph.

a. To show how the average tuition fee for an undergraduate course has changed over the past three decades.   _____

b. To show the number of boxes of popcorn sold at a cinema on a Saturday evening; boxes of popcorn are categorised as 'small', 'medium', 'large' and 'maxi'.   _____

c. To show the proportion of employees in a company who bring a packed lunch, eat their lunch in the staff restaurant or buy lunch from a local shop.   _____

At the end of this unit, you will be able to:
- make comparisons using graphs and charts
- understand the importance of explaining terminology
- summarise your results

Task 1 Comparing qualitative data

A grouped bar chart is a very useful tool if you want to make a comparison between two or more sets of qualitative data on the same diagram. Subcategories of data are grouped together so that similarities and differences can be identified more easily.

Example

In a questionnaire, 400 teenagers were asked about their favourite pizza toppings. The responses are shown in the bar chart below.

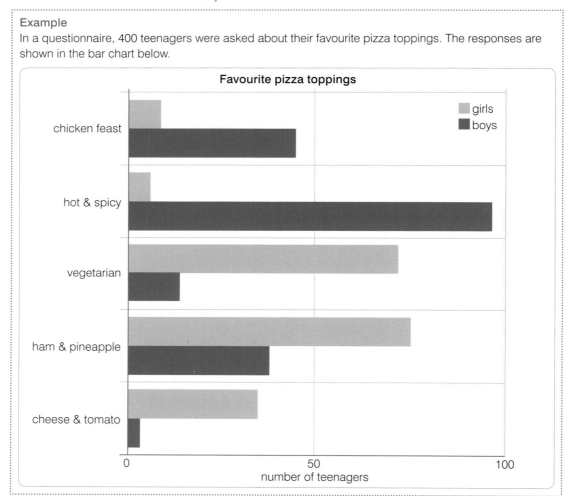

1.1 Using the grouped bar chart shown in the example, decide whether the statements are true (T) or false (F).

a. More girls prefer ham & pineapple pizza topping compared to boys. ☐

b. Chicken feast is the most popular pizza topping amongst the teenage boys who completed the questionnaire. ☐

c. The researcher found that the least popular topping for both genders was cheese & tomato. ☐

d. More boys prefer hot & spicy pizza topping compared to girls. ☐

1.2 The members of selected families were interviewed about the type of books they liked to read while on holiday. Using the grouped bar chart below, write four sentences to describe the similarities and differences in preference between children and adults.

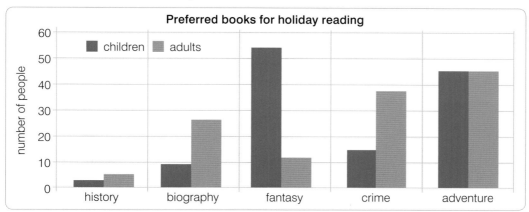

a. _____

_____

b. _____

_____

c. _____

_____

d. _____

_____

6

Task 2 Comparing quantitative data

For comparing several sets of numerical data that change over time, it is best to use a line graph.
You must remember to include a key, also known as a legend, if you are describing more than one data set on the same diagram.

Example

The line graph shows how the average amount of rainfall varies between two cities.

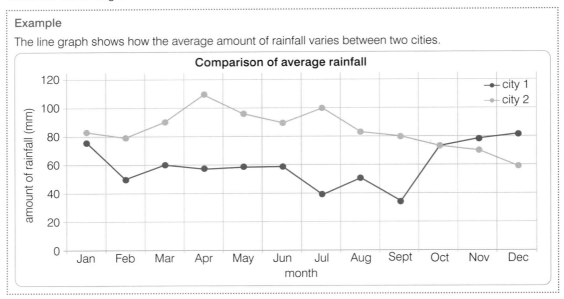

2.1 **Using the line graph shown in the example, answer the questions.**

a. In which month was the average amount of rainfall the same for both cities?

_____

b. Was the month with the most rainfall the same for each city?

_____

c. Which month had the lowest average rainfall in city 1?

_____

d. In which months was the average rainfall lower in city 2 compared to city 1?

_____

2.2 Using the data given in the table, draw a line graph that will allow us to compare the average maximum and minimum temperatures during the year in this city.

month	maximum temperature	minimum temperature
January	25	17
February	25	17
March	24	16
April	23	14
May	20	11
June	16	8
July	15	6
August	17	7
September	20	11
October	21	13
November	24	15
December	26	17

Task 3 Mathematical terminology

The information and tasks in this module have helped you to learn and understand many new words and phrases that have a special meaning in mathematics.

When you are reporting the results of an investigation, it is very important that you explain any specialised vocabulary to your audience regardless of whether you are producing a written report or giving a verbal presentation.

3.1 **Use your own words to write a sentence explaining what is meant by the following mathematical terms. Where appropriate, give an example to support your explanation.**

    a.   variable

        _____

        _____

    b.   sample

        _____

        _____

    c.   mode

        _____

        _____

    d.   line graph

        _____

        _____

Task 4 Summarising results

A complex investigation will often result in the calculation of many different numerical values and the construction of many tables, graphs and charts. This is especially true when you have collected a large amount of data.

Rather than including every calculation and diagram in a report or presentation, you should think carefully about which results are the most meaningful, and which ones your audience are most likely to understand based on their level of knowledge.

Do not forget to include some written interpretation with each diagram and each calculated result so that you can explain what your analysis shows in terms of the specific investigation. There can sometimes be more than one valid conclusion for a set of results.

4.1 **A school Mathematics teacher wanted to find out whether the girls in his class performed better than boys in a Mathematics test. Taking a sample of ten boys and ten girls, he asked them to complete a test that had a maximum score of 100. The table shows his results based on the pupils' scores.**

numerical result	boys	girls
mode score	52	52
mean score	65	71
percentage passed	80%	75%

In your opinion, do the boys in this class perform better or worse than the girls in the Mathematics test, or are their performances the same? Write a short paragraph to explain/ justify your conclusion using some of the numerical results in the table.

4.2 **Compare the paragraph you have written in Task 4.1 with a partner's paragraph. Did you reach the same conclusion?**

    a.   If your conclusions are not the same, discuss whether both conclusions could be valid given the results found in the teacher's investigation.

    b.   If your conclusions are the same, provide an alternative valid conclusion that could also be reached.

Reflect

Find a newspaper, magazine or website article that makes comparisons between men and women in sport. For example, it could be related to competition prize money, race speed, total earnings or television coverage.

Explain to a partner the ways in which the writer uses graphs and numerical values to highlight differences and similarities between the genders. Check if the writer uses any mathematical terminology that they do not fully explain.

Web work

Website 1

World statistics

http://world-statistics.org/

Review

This website provides access to data collected by a wide range of international organisations such as the United Nations and the World Bank. The user interface is easy to use and results can be displayed in a table or as a graph or chart.

Task

a.   Click on 'Indicators' in the top right menu.

b.   Explore the data provided for different topic areas. Select a topic that you find interesting, for example, 'Environment and Energy', and then continue to choose from the options provided.

c.   Choose several countries and compare their data using the tabulated results and the diagrams available.

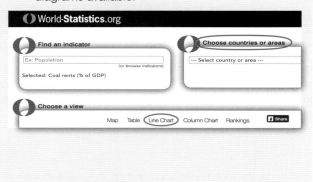

Website 2

Careers using numerical skills

https://nationalcareersservice.direct.gov.uk/

Review

This website provides information and guidance to help people make decisions on learning, training and work opportunities. It helps with advice on how to write a CV, how to identify your strengths and how to choose a career.

Task

Under the 'Careers advice' heading, choose 'Job profiles'. Browse through some of the careers that interest you and write a list of the job profiles that require good numerical skills.

Extension activities

Activity 1

The BBC radio show 'More or Less' aims to explain how numbers and statistics can be applied to everyday life and issues currently in the news. It has attempted to answer questions such as: 'Can you have too much pocket money?' and 'Does a plastic bag really take 1,000 years to decompose?'

With a small group of students, listen to an episode of the show on a subject that interests you and decide whether an entertaining radio show is a good way to introduce numerical analysis to people.

You can access podcasts of the show using: http://www.bbc.co.uk/podcasts/series/moreorless.

Activity 2

Work with a partner to choose a topic that is relevant to your lifestyle, such as shopping, studying, leisure activities, using social media or sport, and carry out a small scale investigation. Your investigation should include the following stages of work as described in Unit 2:

1. Write a short questionnaire, making sure you collect both quantitative and qualitative data. Check Unit 3 for some ideas of open and closed questions. Ask ten friends or family members to complete the questionnaire.

2. Use some of the techniques described in Units 4 and 5 to analyse the data you have collected. It is important that you try to construct tables, draw diagrams and perform some numerical calculations. Identify any patterns and highlight any interesting features in your data set.

3. With reference to some of the comparison methods in Unit 6, discuss the conclusions that you can reach based on the graphical and numerical results.

4. Prepare slides for a short presentation that describes your investigation. Explain your data collection methods, the techniques you used for analysis and the conclusions reached.

Glossary

analysis (n) The use of diagrams and numerical values to highlight interesting features.

attribute (n) A characteristic used to describe a person or an object, for example, height or colour.

average (n) A typical value that is representative of a set of data you have collected. The three types are the mode, the median and the mean.

axes (n) Plural of the noun *axis*.

axis (n) A reference line used to locate a point on a graph.

bar chart (n) The graphical display of data using vertical or horizontal rectangular bars.

biased (adj) A prejudice for or against something. For example, a sample of data which does not properly represent the population from which it was chosen.

category (n) A group with shared characteristics.

characteristic (n) A distinguishing quality or feature of a person or an object.

chart (n) A set of data in the form of a graph or diagram.

classify (v) To arrange data in categories depending on shared characteristics.

closed question (n) A question which provides a fixed number of answers from which the participant must choose.

comparison (n) A way of analysing the similarities or differences between two things.

conclusion (n) A final judgement based on a completed investigation.

continuous variable (n) A variable that can take any numerical value within a specific range.

data (n) A type of information collected for reference or analysis.

data set (n) A collection of related data.

decimal number (n) A number with one or more digits on the right side of the decimal point, which is another way of representing a fraction.

decimal point (n) A full point or dot to represent the units of a decimal number.

decrease (n) (v) 1 (n) The amount by which something has become smaller. 2 (v) To grow smaller in number, amount or intensity.

diagram (n) A chart or graph used to display data values.

digit (n) Any number from 0 to 9.

discrete variable (n) A variable that can take only specific numerical values.

display (v) To present something, for example, a set of data in a graph.

exact (adj) Accurate information.

finite (adj) A limited amount.

fraction (n) A numerical quantity that is not a whole number.

frequency (n) The number of times that a specific value occurs in a set of data.

frequency table (n) A way of displaying collected data values and their corresponding frequencies.

gender (n) A state of being male or female.

graph (n) A diagram which shows the relationship between different quantities.

grouped bar chart (n) A way of making a comparison between two or more sets of data on the same bar chart.

guidelines (n) A set of rules for a course of action.

horizontally (adv) To put something parallel to the horizon.

image (n) A picture of a person or object.

increase (n) (v) 1 (n) The amount by which something has become larger. 2 (v) To grow larger in number, amount, or intensity.

interpretation (n) An explanation of what your analysis shows in terms of your specific investigation.

interview (n) (v) 1 (n) A formal meeting of people, usually with one asking the other questions for a specific purpose. 2 (v) To hold an interview.

key (n) Also known as a legend; an explanation of the symbols used in a graph or diagram.

label (n) (v) 1 (n) A phrase or name applied to an object or thing. 2 (v) To attach a label to something.

legend (n) Also known as a key; an explanation of the symbols used in a graph or diagram.

line graph (n) A graphical display used to present quantitative data that changes over time.

mean (n) A type of average where the sum of the data values is divided by the number of data values collected.

median (n) A type of average which finds the middle value for a set of data that is arranged in numerical order.

mode (n) A type of average which finds the data value that occurs most frequently.

open question (n) A question where the person can give any response they choose.

participant (n) The person answering questions for research purposes.

percentage (n) A proportion or number expressed as a fraction of 100.

pie chart (n) A circular diagram that is used for displaying proportions for qualitative data.

population (n) The entire set of people from whom a researcher may wish to collect information.

present (v) To show or display information to other people.

proportion (n) A section of data taken from a whole.

qualitative variable (n) A characteristic that cannot be described using numbers; letters or words are used instead.

quantitative variable (n) A characteristic that can be described using numerical values.

questionnaire (n) A list of questions that is used to collect data from people.

recurring (adj) Occurs repeatedly, for example, digits in a recurring decimal number are repeated endlessly.

relationship (n) The way in which two or more things are connected, for example, different sets of data.

representative (adj) Follows the typical opinions of the group in question.

researcher (n) A person who conducts research on a specific matter.

sample (n) A small group of people selected from a population.

sampling (n) The selection of a sample group from a population.

scale (n) A standard measurement.

scatter diagram (n) A diagram used to display information about two quantitative variables that might be connected in some way.

segment (n) One of the parts or portions into which something can be divided.

simplify (v) To make something simpler or easier to understand.

statistics (n) A mathematical science that generally involves the collection, analysis, interpretation and presentation of data.

subcategory (n) A smaller group within a category with shared characteristics.

summarise (v) To give a brief statement of the main points.

table (n) A set of data values displayed systematically, usually in columns.

tabulate (v) To arrange data values in a table.

terminology (n) Specialised vocabulary from a particular subject.

three-dimensional (adj) An object with height, width and depth.

two-way table (n) A way of displaying collected data values for two qualitative variables with their corresponding frequencies.

valid (adj) (of a point) Having a sound basis in logic or fact.

value (n) A numerical quantity.

variable (n) A characteristic or an attribute that can have different values.

vertically (adv) To put something at a right angle to the horizon.

Notes

Notes

Published by
Garnet Publishing Ltd
8 Southern Court
South Street
Reading RG1 4QS, UK

ISBN 978 1 78260 185 2

British Library Cataloguing-in-Publication Data
A catalogue record for this book is available from the British Library.

Production

Project manager:	Clare Chandler
Editorial team:	Clare Chandler, Matthew George, Kate Kemp
Design & layout:	Madeleine Maddock
Photography:	iStockphoto

Garnet Publishing and the authors of TASK would like to thank the staff and students of the International Foundation Programme at the University of Reading for their respective roles in the development of these teaching materials.

All website URLs provided in this publication were correct at the time of printing. If any URL does not work, please contact your tutor, who will help you find similar resources.

Printed and bound in Lebanon by International Press: interpress@int-press.com

Acknowledgements
Page 34: Web work, Website 1, Screenshot of World Statistics website, reproduced with kind permission